The World of Composers

Wagner

Greta Cencetti

PETER BEDRICK BOOKS

McGraw-Hill
Children's Publishing
A Division of The **McGraw·Hill** Companies

This edition published in the United States in 2002 by
Peter Bedrick Books, an imprint of
McGraw-Hill Children's Publishing,
A Division of The McGraw-Hill Companies
8787 Orion Place
Columbus, Ohio 43240

www.MHkids.com

ISBN 1-58845-474-6

Library of Congress Cataloging-in-Publication Data

Cencetti, Greta.
Wagner / Greta Cencetti.
p. cm. -- (The world of composers)
Summary: Describes the life and career of the nineteenth-century composer
considered by many to be the master of German opera.
ISBN 1-58845-474-6
1. Wagner, Richard, 1813-1883--Juvenile literature. 2. Composers—Germany—
Biography—Juvenile literature. [1. Wagner, Richard, 1813-1883.
2. Composers.] I. Title. II. Series.

ML3930.W2 C36 2002
782.1'092--dc21
[B]
2001052905

10 9 8 7 6 5 4 3 2 1 CHRT 06 05 04 03 02

Printed in China.

The World of Composers

Wagner

Greta Cencetti

PETER BEDRICK BOOKS

Contents

Leipzig

Chapter 1
The Young Richard Wagner

Richard Wagner (pronounced VAHG-nuhr) was born on May 22, 1813, in Leipzig, Germany. His father was a police officer, who died in November of that same year. Ludwig Geyer, a family friend, married Wagner's mother shortly after she was widowed. Geyer introduced his wife to literature, art, and theater. The family moved to Dresden, Germany, where Ludwig was offered a position to schedule performances at the Hoftheater, an opera house. Although Geyer died when Wagner was only eight years old, his stepfather's involvement in music had a lifelong effect on him.

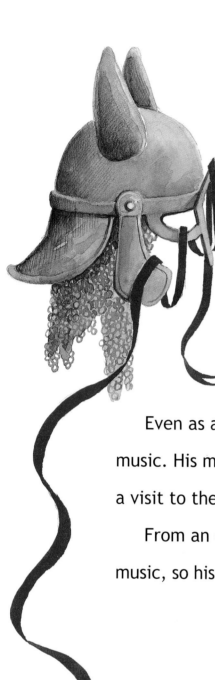

Even as a baby, Wagner seemed to love theater and music. His mother noticed that he burst into laughter upon a visit to the opera house.

From an early age, Wagner expressed a desire to learn music, so his parents encouraged him to take piano lessons.

Wagner began to write scripts and compose songs when he was just a young boy. Although Wagner was musically talented, he did not respond well to discipline. His family struggled to get Richard to take school seriously.

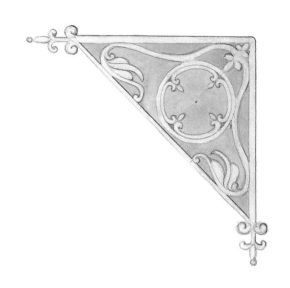

Chapter 2
A Life of Luxury

As Wagner grew up, he became restless. Constantly on the move, he traveled throughout Europe. After Wagner returned home from a trip to Prague, he started composing his first opera, *Die Feen* (The Fairies).

At the time, opera was a popular musical form. Wagner worked in several German cities as an opera conductor. He seemed to find work easily and lived the luxurious lifestyle he wanted with the money he earned.

Wagner stood out because he loved fine things and was fond of fancy clothes. He particularly enjoyed wearing hats. Sometimes Wagner's love of expensive things got him into trouble. He often owed money for the things he bought.

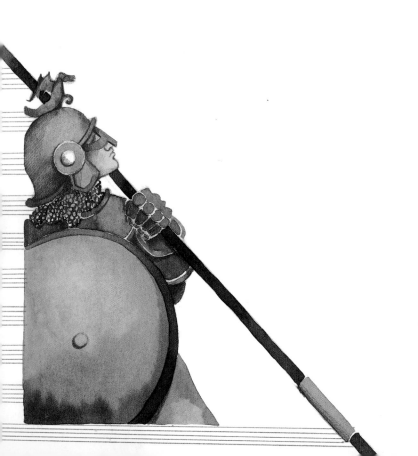

Chapter 3
The Actress and the Composer

When Wagner was 23, he accepted a job as musical director of a traveling theater company. There, he met a young actress named Christine Wilhelmine ("Minna") Planer. They fell in love and married a short time later.

In the years that followed, Wagner not only conducted an orchestra and a choir, but he also composed many songs. Even though he had married, he continued his travels.

In 1838, when Wagner was 25, he was invited to go to Northern Europe to manage the opera house in Riga. The Wagners stayed there for a year, but fell heavily in debt.

Wagner was nearly put in prison because he always spent more money than he had. He owed money to several shopkeepers, the tailor, and the owners of fancy restaurants. Wagner and his wife's debts became overwhelming, and they decided to flee from Riga.

Chapter 4
The Power of Nature

One dark evening, Wagner and his wife secretly boarded a ship because their passports had been taken. They sailed from Riga to London. During the trip, their ship was pounded by a heavy rainstorm. Wagner feared for their lives, but the ship arrived safely in England.

Wagner's experience with the storm inspired him to write a series of musical works. These pieces are found in the opera *The Flying Dutchman*. This opera tells the tale of a captain who is cursed to wander the seas throughout time.

Chapter 5
Fairy Tales, Legends, and Great Music

Wagner ended up in France, where things got so bad that he spent several weeks in a debtor's prison. Even so, music continued to inspire him. A short time later, Wagner was introduced by a German friend to two German legends, Tannhäuser and Lohengrin. Wagner soon developed a love for German mythology. This interest influenced his later operas. The dramatic stories of ancient heroes and warriors inspired him to write a new kind of opera, full of rich, fantastic sounds and beautiful continuous melody.

Wagner visited Paris and London before returning to Dresden. There, he was appointed conductor of the opera. He created two of his most successful operas during this time, *Tannhäuser* and *Lohengrin*. *Tannhäuser* tells the story of a knight whose heart is torn between the love for two women. *Lohengrin* is about another knight, who defends and marries the Duke's daughter, Elsa. At the end of the opera, brave Lohengrin is forced to leave a brokenhearted Elsa.

Chapter 6
Admiration From the King

After settling down for a while in Dresden, Wagner became restless again and set out for Switzerland and France. He returned to Germany when Ludwig II was crowned king of Bavaria in Southern Germany.

Ludwig II played an important role in Wagner's life. He was a great admirer of the composer's music. Not only was Ludwig a friend to Wagner, but he provided him with monetary support. Ludwig gave Wagner a country home. He later built him an opera house to show his admiration.

Despite the fact that Ludwig made Wagner so welcome in Germany, he was still a wanderer. He continued to travel throughout Europe.

Chapter 7

Divorce and a New Romance

Wagner's interests in European legends led him to compose some of his most moving operas. Wagner believed that opera should combine all forms of art. He was the first composer to create this new form of opera.

Although Wagner was excited about his work, he was not happy in his marriage. Wagner and Minna had many differences. In 1862, they divorced.

Although Wagner was saddened by the separation, he found comfort in the love of another. He met a young woman named Cosima von Bülow. She was the daughter of the well-known musician and composer, Franz Liszt.

Despite a great difference in their ages, Cosima and Wagner fell deeply in love and married. The public did not approve of their marriage, but the two were extremely happy. They were always welcome at the palace of Ludwig II. They had a child, Isolde, on April 10, 1865. Two more children followed, Cosima in 1867 and Siegfried in 1869.

Chapter 8
Wagner Sets the Trend

*W*agner made several important changes to the way opera was received. The opera houses of the time were built in the shape of a semicircle and were lit by candlelight. The orchestra was seated in a lower area, facing the audience.

During Wagner's time, the audience did not show much respect for the performers. They walked around eating, drinking, and talking during the performance. It was hard for the performers to hold their attention.

Wagner did not like this casual atmosphere. He insisted that the candles be put out during a performance, leaving the audience in total darkness. This encouraged members of the audience to remain seated and attentive. Those who would not cooperate were asked to leave. Respectful audience behavior soon became the standard in opera houses everywhere.

Ludwig II continued to support Wagner. Festspielhaus, the opera house that Ludwig built for Wagner, opened in Bayreuth in 1876. Four days before the official opening, one of Wagner's operas was performed. This opera was called *Der Ring Des Nibelungen* (*The Ring of the Nibelung*), and is based on one of the most famous German legends about the powerful god Wotan.

Der Ring Des Nibelungen was very popular and helped to make Wagner one of the most important composers in Europe.

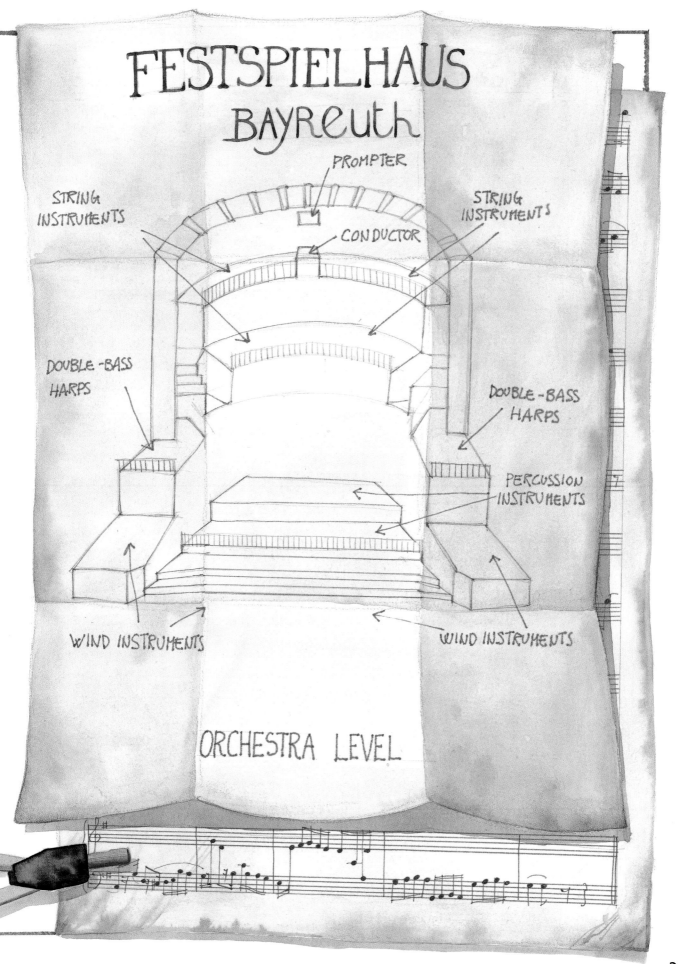

Chapter 9
Wagner's Final Years

Later in his life, Wagner settled down. In 1882, after five years, he finished his final opera, *Parsifal*.

Wagner spent his last years in Venice, Italy. He loved the magical architecture and beauty of the city. He had a fatal heart attack there on February 13, 1883, at the age of 70.

Wagner's operas, with their rich music and stories, continue to be enjoyed by audiences throughout the world. One of Wagner's biggest achievements was his success in encouraging audiences to support and appreciate musical performers and their works.

Introduction to Wind Instruments

$\mathcal{T}$he opera uses an orchestra as musical background to its performances of singing and acting. An important part of an orchestra is a group of instruments known as wind instruments.

Wind instruments come in a variety of shapes and sizes, and are made from wood or metal. To produce a sound, a player blows through a mouthpiece, and the air vibrates through the column of the instrument. Opening and closing different combinations of keys on the column changes the length of the column and thus the pitch of the instrument.

There are two categories of wind instruments: brass and woodwind. Brass instruments have metal mouthpieces into which the player buzzes his or her lips. Brass instruments include the trumpet, the trombone, the French horn, the tuba, and the cornet. The woodwinds include the flute, piccolo, oboe, English horn, clarinet, bass clarinet, bassoon, contrabassoon, and saxophones. With the exception of the flute and the piccolo, woodwinds have mouthpieces that use a reed. A reed is a strip of cane that the player causes to vibrate by blowing on it, making a sound similar to a New Year's noisemaker or Halloween horn. The flute and piccolo make their sounds by having a player blow over an opening in the instrument, like blowing over the top of a bottle.

Wagner made wonderful use of the woodwinds and brasses in his operas, producing sounds from the orchestra that no one had heard before—sounds that described the fantastic, mysterious world of German mythology. Wagner even had a new instrument made for his orchestra and named for him: the Wagner tuba. This special tuba gave his works a richer, fuller sound, filling in a gap where other instruments could not play.